Jawaharlal Nehru

Sumitha Menon

Jawaharlal Nehru
© *New Horizon Media*

First Edition: July 2009
64 Pages
Printed in India.

ISBN 978–81–8493–194–5

Pro–ya–en–47

Prodigy Books
177/103, First Floor, Ambal's Building
Lloyds Road, Royapettah, Chennai 600 014.
Ph: +91-44-4200-9603
Email: support@nhm.in
Website: www.nhm.in

Prodigy Books is an imprint of New Horizon Media Pvt. Ltd.

Content

The 'Gem' of Anand Bhavan

Pandit Jawaharlal Nehru, was a charismatic personality, powerful yet revered, warm yet aristocratic, honest yet tolerant, and was one of the greatest leaders in twentieth-century Asia.

Jawaharlal was born on 14 November, 1889 at Allahabad, as the eldest child to Motilal Nehru and Swarup Rani. He was a Kashmiri Brahmin, an upper caste Hindu. His father, Motilal Nehru, was one of the most distinguished lawyers and richest men in India. Highly influential both socially and politically, Motilal was a learned scholar who excelled in several languages, including Persian, Urdu, Arabic and English. Nehru and his entire family lived at 'Anand Bhavan' in Allahabad. The house has been preserved to this day, as a monument.

'Jawahar' means 'gem' in Arabic. Little Jawahar grew up in luxury at the family's palatial estate, with a private swimming pool, tennis court, riding stables and magnificent gardens. His two sisters, Vijaya Lakshmi Pandit and Krishna Pandit, were 11 years younger to him. So he grew up as a lonely affluent child, pampered with love and affection. He had a happy upbringing, though in Westernised surroundings — in customs, manners and dress sense.

However, his mother assured an Indian environment at home. She practised several Hindu customs and narrated folklore to little Jawahar. He picked up a lot of legends from women in his family, regularly went to the temple and took a holy dip in the Ganges. His father, Motilal Nehru, was neither very religious-minded nor was he an atheist. However, he paid great attention to every minute detail with regard to his son. He wanted for his son the best that British education could give. So Jawaharlal initially had two governesses, was later sent to a local convent for a few months, till finally his father settled on private tuitions for Jawahar at home.

A great Sanskrit scholar, Pandit Ganganatha Jha, tried to teach Jawaharlal Sanskrit but with little success. FT Brooks, a young Irish-French theosophist, taught him from 1901 to1904. Under his tutorship, Jawaharlal got an insight into English poetry and literature. Brooks also developed in him an interest in science, by making a tiny make-shift laboratory in his room. Jawaharlal regularly listened to Brook's discourses on theosophy and realised that there was more to religion than myth and miracle. Even epics like Upanishads and Bhagavat Gita were read by him at Brook's insistence, though he could not comprehend it fully at that time.

Motilal, however, was not satisfied with mere private tuitions for his son and with Brooks. So in 1905, he sought admission for his son at Harrow for higher studies. Jawaharlal was 16 then. Though slim and not very tall, he was fair and handsome with finely sculpted features and aquiline nose. His well-brushed black hair was already on the thin side. As a young man dressed in Western attire, he looked more like an Englishman rather than an Indian.

He was good at his school work, and was therefore in the good books of his teachers. While Jawaharlal was in Harrow, India was going through an eventful period, and for the first time he began to show interest in politics and world affairs. In 1905, the partitioning of the Province of Bengal by Viceroy Lord Curzon resulted in agitations in Bengal and won support from other parts of India. There was awareness that it was done to weaken the growing feeling of Indian nationalism. Jawaharlal was a keen observer of news and asked his father to send him Indian newspapers regularly.

Bored with Harrow, Jawaharlal took the entrance examination to Cambridge in 1907, and went to Trinity in October. Jawaharlal, in his letters to his father, showed his support to the extremists who believed in agitation in India, but he did not take part in the student politics of Cambridge. There were no signs of any fire or interest in him to fight against the values and ambitions upheld by his class of society. He did not resist, when his father wanted him to appear for the ICS examination. At that time, neither the father nor the son had any dislike in serving the British rulers. They both had never felt the need for freedom at that time.

Cambridge was an exciting place in those days. Jawaharlal had taken up chemistry, geology and physics as his subjects but soon exchanged physics for botany, and secured only a second class in the final examination. It was not in keeping with his talent and Jawaharlal was also not academically inclined. He did not work hard in his studies and was extremely shy too. While in Cambridge, he was in the debating team and often paid fine for not speaking up for an entire term.

He was, however, very active outside the laboratories and lecture rooms. Robust in health, he loved active sports such as skiing, swimming, mountain climbing and horse riding. He also practised hatha-yoga. He also played tennis, joined the Trinity Boat Club and even indulged in gambling.

Jawaharlal Nehru had many acquaintances but none of his friends was intimate. He did not make friends with the women too. Loneliness engulfed him at times and his pursuit of pleasures was a means to cover up the emptiness in his life.

Even before his final examinations he had joined Law, which made his father very happy. He was sure that his son would do well. However, in reality, Jawaharlal had no interest in Law; he had joined the course as a pastime. He was just pulling along idly, with no purpose in life.

Meanwhile, he met with a near-fatal accident. While on holiday with a friend in Norway, he was trekking somewhere north of Bergen; he got into an ice-cold fjord (submerged 'U'-shaped glaciated valley or a deep inlet from the sea bordered by steep hills) for a bath and became numb. His foot slipped, and he was carried away by the current. His friend pulled him out from the mouth of a waterfall. But Jawaharlal was a man of courage and valour and enjoyed such risks.

For the next two years, Jawaharlal plunged into London life in full swing. He renewed his contact with some old school acquaintances and became the most fashionable man—an elegant, charming, young intellectual and a socialite. He enthusiastically took part in the political activities of the Indian student community. A regular at the theatres, museums and opera houses of London, he would spend his vacation touring Europe. Obviously, it ran him into debt and he had to pawn his watch and chain. Sometimes, he had no money even for bus or tube (the British subway) fares and approached his father for more money.

His father, Motilal Nehru, was in for a shock. Leave alone scholarships or prizes at the Bar examinations, Jawaharlal had only managed to get a pass. He had been an obedient son doing whatever he had been asked to do, but did not show any particular enthusiasm in any subject. His attachment to his father had made him passive, leaving all the major decisions of his life to his father. His traditional education at England for seven long years did nothing to boost his confidence or induce interest in the world. Many would have been disappointed that he did not shine academically as he had done in Harrow but Jawaharlal had no regrets. He returned to India with a sharper mind and enriched imagination. His mind and character had not been trained for any profession but he was well prepared for a call that came later.

Certain values that he considered British never left him. They guided his outlook, supported him in his struggles and influenced him in his policies while in power.

Young Nehru

In India, Nehru slipped into the daily routine of the upper middle-class society with ease. He joined his father's office and worked fairly hard. Though he had the advantage of his father's name and social contacts with judges, eminent lawyers, landlords and industrialists, he did not develop any interest in law.

In Allahabad, Jawaharlal continued to lead the hectic social life of London. Motilal was a stylish man; he had a luxurious life and entertained lavishly. Nehru enjoyed his father's social gatherings and organised his own late-night parties and revelry. Motilal was also an active member of the Indian National Congress and this helped in shaping up Jawaharlal's political life. His father maintained extremely cordial relations with the British officers. He had faith in British justice and British promises, and in many instances supported the British officers. He extended his hospitality to the British officers and they, in turn, respected the Nehru family and welcomed them to their homes. This kind of family meetings gave Jawaharlal and his sisters a glimpse of the British lifestyle. There was no discrimination between the son and the daughters. As we shall see later, they were all provided with good education and given equal privileges. Both the sisters participated actively in family affairs and politics as well. They supported Jawaharlal, and he in turn influenced them in their political career and personal life.

Motilal very broad-minded. There were no class restrictions in the Nehru household. He kept an open house for people of all castes and religions. Servants who worked at 'Anand Bhavan' were of different castes and religion.

Even when Jawharlal was in Harrow, Motilal Nehru and his wife were searching for a perfect match for their son. After a long search, in 1912, they chose Kamala Kaul — a young girl of 13 from a Kashmiri middle-class family. After the engagement, she was brought to Allahabad for training in necessary etiquette. When she was 17, the wedding took place on a grand scale in Delhi.

The first few years of their married life had their own hurdles because of the cultural divide between the anglicised Nehru and the homely Kamala, who followed

Hindu traditions and had only her family's interest at heart. Kamala gave birth to their only daughter Indira Priyadarshini in 1917.

Though he continued his legal practice, Nehru was getting attracted to Indian politics. Indian politicians were demanding Home Rule and Dominion Status for India. However, he did not know what sort of action should be taken, or what kind of non-cooperation should be executed. So, in his late twenties, Jawaharlal was a discontented man, who could not make up his own mind and was feeling rather uncomfortable with all the luxuries and affluence. He became disillusioned with the liberal and anglicised approach of the Congress politicians, including his father. He craved for action, which would give him mental and emotional satisfaction. So when Gandhi's call came, he responded willingly.

Years later, he said that it was the 'acceptance of Gandhi's leadership and the civil disobedience and jail-going which had followed that had made a man of him.' His life now had a meaning.

Entry into Politics

Jawaharlal was attracted to Gandhi's philosophy and leadership. Along with Gandhi, he pledged refusal to obey certain rules and formed a committee to organise *Satyagraha* — mass civil disobedience, governed by *Ahimsa* or complete non-violence. He also helped in relief work after the Amritsar (Jalianwala Bagh) massacre by General Dyer. Till then, he was expecting the British rulers to relent and favour them, but later realised that freedom would never be gifted to them; it had to be won by struggle and resistance.

Jawaharlal's acceptance of Gandhi's austere way of life, in fact, pained Motilal, because for him austerity and puritanism did not come naturally. The father and son had misunderstandings on that score but Jawaharlal was keen in following Gandhi's leadership. He plunged deeply into the task of organising non-cooperation movement in UP. What appealed to Jawaharlal were Gandhi's strength and his commitment to India's freedom — his personality and character, restlessness and energy, eagerness to act — all impressed young Jawaharlal.

Jawaharlal's involvement in the peasant's unrest in UP was a milestone in his political career. The 'Rent Act of 1886' prevented landlords from enhancing rent by more than one anna (16 annas made one rupee) once in seven years. The landlords, to make up for their loss, began demanding higher taxes in addition to the rent, or the farmers faced eviction. Naturally, there was a growing resentment amongst the peasants. Their leaders called upon them to stand up for their rights and resist the landlords, pay rent but not illegal taxes. About 500 farmers came to Allahabad, hoping to meet Gandhi; they instead met Jawaharlal who happened to be there. Thus, circumstances led to his getting involved in the cause of the peasants. The peaceful yet firm attitude of these men, who, though poor, never let themselves to be suppressed, overwhelmed him.

He gave voice to the *kisans'* (farmer in Hindi) grievances. He encouraged the peasants to organise themselves into village *kisan sabhas* and formulate their demands. In Rae Bareli and Pratapgarh, he advised them to boycott elections to the councils. He wanted to link the *kisan* discontent with the non-cooperation movement. However, the unjust attitude of the landlords and the reckless handling of the situation in UP enhanced the peasant's unrest, and there was spurt of violence in Rae Bareli and other districts.

Realising the seriousness of the situation, Jawaharlal visited Rae Bareli but was asked by the deputy commissioner to leave the place at once. Indignant at this unjust order, Nehru refused to go back. He told the farmers whom he came across to be both non-violent and fearless. Since he was reminded again that meetings were prohibited he dissolved the meeting and the crowd dispersed. He visited the wounded in the hospital along with his father, the next day. The whole incident was an experience that affected Jawaharlal deeply. His influence bordered on moderation, and urged the farmers to be quiet and peaceful.

In November 1921, the All India Congress Committee (AICC) permitted full Civil Disobedience, including non-payment of taxes (but not of rents).

Gandhi's disciple

Jawaharlal appealed to the students to leave government schools and colleges and to serve as volunteers — either to help the farmers or to spin the wheel. He suggested that at least 50,000 people from the district should be registered as Congress members. Special efforts were made to enlist women.

Following Gandhi's example, Nehru and his family gave up their Western-style dresses, possessions and luxurious lifestyle. He advocated the boycott of foreign cloth. In Allahabad city, he, along with the others, went round collecting foreign clothes from each house. He believed that the attainment of *swaraj* (Self-government) depended on the use of *swadeshi* cloth. People should discard or burn foreign stuff and use home-made cloth instead.

At the same time, he was not defiant. He abided by the rules of the government. At Shikarpur, he was served an order prohibiting the meeting wherein he was speaking. He immediately stopped his speech and began to collect foreign clothes and subscriptions for the *swaraj* fund. In another place, when such an order was given, he marched with the whole audience, numbering about a thousand, to the next district four-and-a-half miles away and held the meeting there.

The UP government, in the meantime, was collecting evidence to take action against Jawaharlal for his speeches, and against his father's newspaper *Independent* for its articles. In November 1921, the Government of India decided to take drastic action against the non-cooperation campaign. Also the volunteer movement was declared unlawful. Jawaharlal, its secretary, and his father were arrested for their involvement in its activities.

The two were happy to go to prison and welcomed the sentence of six month's simple imprisonment and a fine of Rs.100 or one more month in jail. Jawaharlal considered it a trophy for his patriotism. Both father and son were given better treatment than the ordinary Congress workers but they declined the privileges. Jawaharlal continued to guide the working of the Congress from prison. To his surprise, however, he was released from jail when he had served only half the term.

By then, Gandhi had called off the civil disobedience campaign, because of the increasing violence. Jawaharlal was a bit disappointed since the movement was gaining strength in his province. He addressed public meetings, and organised spinning, boycott and picketing in UP. On May 12, he was again arrested for organising picketing and supporting it in his articles and speeches. Jawaharlal argued that the government was responsible for oppression and terrorism. He said he was glad that their action had given publicity to the boycott of foreign cloth.

In fact, his trial statements won him a national audience and it became the manifesto of the educated youth. However, he was sentenced to a rigorous imprisonment of 18 months and a fine of Rs.100 or a further three months' jail. Jawaharlal enjoyed his stay in prison. The confinement itself boosted his self-respect. He hoped that the tough life there would harden him. He spent his enforced leisure by exercising — walking and running, spinning every day and mostly reading. His favourite subjects were history, travel and romantic poetry. Again, he was set free before serving his full sentence, on 31 January, 1923.

When he came out of prison, what hit him was the sharp difference of opinion within the Congress itself. With Gandhi in jail, he tried to convince the Congress leadership that the differences would only weaken the organisation as a whole. He was made one of the executive members of the party. But in Nagpur, in July, the AICC rejected Jawaharlal's resolution to take disciplinary action against the undisciplined members. He, along with his colleagues, resigned from the working committee and expressed their desire to resign from the AICC as well.

Jawaharlal was now a free man. He realised that mass civil disobedience was out of question for the time being, but he helped organise the *satyagraha* in Nagpur, when the district magistrate refused permission to a Congress procession, to carry the national flag. Finally, the authorities had to give in and allowed the procession.

He was by then attracted by the activities of the Akali Dal in Punjab. He wanted to see for himself the Akalis in action. So he entered Nabha state on 21 September, 1923, to support the agitation of Akalis. He was arrested along with his companions, and locked up in jail.

The condition of Nabha jail was terrible. The prisoners were not allowed to see or communicate with anyone outside. No books or papers were given to them and there was no permission even to bathe and change for two days. The authorities altered the charges to suit their convenience and the case dragged on. Motilal came to see his son in jail but Jawaharlal was irritated at his father's intervention. Motilal was upset and went away. Jawaharlal and his two companions were sentenced to 30 months' rigorous imprisonment. The sentence, however, was suspended and they were ordered to leave Nabha and not to return. Jawaharlal and others left the town the same night.

On his return to Allahabad Jawaharlal was welcomed like a hero. However, he was down with typhoid and felt very feeble. His father too saw to it that Jawahar did not involve himself in the affairs of Nabha again.

His ill-health now prevented him from being physically present at all meetings. But he wrote the speeches that were to be read in his absence. His speeches reiterated the need for peaceful pursuits. He wrote, 'The choice for us is between Lenin and Mussolini on the one side and Gandhi on the other. Can there be any doubt as to who represents the soul of India today?' To Jawaharlal, non-violent non-cooperation was a positive programme and its champion (Gandhi) a man of action.

At this time, Jawaharlal was thrust into many administrative duties, which kept him very busy. Meanwhile, Gandhi was released on account of health problems. In September 1924, the growing communal disharmony prompted Gandhi to go on a fast for 21 days.

For Jawaharlal, these months were also a phase of stress and depression. In November 1924, his wife lost a child after premature birth and soon developed symptoms of tuberculosis. In 1925, he had to undergo a minor operation.

His commitment to Gandhi and adherence to *swaraj* policy had caused friction between him and his father.

His difference of opinion with his father made Jawaharlal aware of his acute dependence on his father for money. Gandhi offered to find him some work so that he could earn some money. Jawaharlal was not ready to work for any commercial firm. Finally, he began to practise law, though he disliked it. He needed some money to travel to Europe with Kamala.

He also became the chairman of the Allahabad Municipal Council. He encouraged the wearing of *Khaddar* by municipal employees and the use of Hindi or Urdu in official transactions. His moderate and impartial actions gave Jawaharlal a commanding influence. He managed to introduce spinning and weaving in schools. He was keen to improve the quality of education in municipal schools, raise the salaries of teachers and train children to be good citizens. Scouting was introduced for boys. He brought about a lot of reforms for the welfare of the people and municipality. His work attracted wide public attention. Even the commissioner was impressed and gave full credit to Jawaharlal for all the improvements in the administration.

In Europe (1926–1927)

On 1 March, 1926, Jawaharlal sailed with his wife and daughter to Europe. The journey was mainly undertaken for Kamala, hoping that a long stay in Switzerland would cure her of tuberculosis. The two years did Kamala no good, but it had a deep impact on Jawaharlal's mental development.

In India, the Congress was laden with dissension and communal tension was rising. Gandhi was still hopeful. The news from India depressed Jawaharlal. Settled in Geneva's cheap lodgings, he nursed his wife, escorted his daughter to school and back, learnt French, read widely and attended various courses and lectures.

By the end of the year, there was no improvement in Kamala's condition. Jawaharlal was getting restless and longed for the wider world and India. However, his wife was still unwell and Motilal was also planning a trip to the West. So the family began a tour of Europe. During these travels, he came in contact with European political workers and movements, which took his thinking and activities to new depths.

He was invited to organise and participate, as the representative of the Indian National Congress, in the International Congress against Colonial Oppression and Imperialism to be held at Brussels in February 1927. He was the only delegate from India and played a leading role in drafting many resolutions. He pointed out that the policy of the British was to create differences among Indians. His resolution on India gained immense support for the liberation of India from foreign domination and all kinds of exploitation.

A joint declaration of Indian and Chinese delegates drafted by Jawaharlal recalled the close cultural ties between India and China for over 3,000 years and blamed the British for nurturing ill-will against India in China. The Brussels Conference decided to find a League against Imperialism and for National Independence, in order to organise co-operation between nationalist movements in the colonial countries. Jawaharlal was appointed honorary president of the League and a member of the executive committee. During his stay in Europe for the rest of the year, he attended the meeting of the executive committee regularly.

Jawaharlal was impressed by the developments and conditions in the Soviet Union. He decided that though India was opposed to Communism she could have friendly relations with Russia. He made up his mind to visit the Soviet Union before returning to India. The opportunity presented itself when Motilal and he were invited to the decennial celebrations of the 1917 Revolution.

They were in Russia only for a few days, but the articles Jawaharlal wrote showed his deep commitment towards the country. He knew that they were seeing only what they were allowed to see. However, he was sure that the Soviet Union had made tremendous progress in agriculture, prison reforms, literacy, treatment of women, and in bridging the rich-poor divide. He knew that the Soviet Union had a lot to teach India, which was also an agricultural country laden with poverty and illiteracy.

Jawaharlal returned to India as a revolutionary, influenced by what he saw, heard and read in Europe. Though he remained dedicated to Gandhian principles, he was never again bound by them. Jawaharlal always had a fascination for the European tradition, wanting to apply and adapt its doctrine in his own country.

Campaigning for Independence

Jawaharlal was convinced that the aim of the Congress party should be nothing less than total independence. He was not in favour of the assent of the Congress for Dominion Status. He could not accept the argument that there was no difference between Dominion Status and Independence. Dominion Status demanded the maintenance of a connection with Britain, who will exercise her authority in all fields. Independence, however, need not mean enmity with Britain. India could co-operate with Britain on an equal footing. Agreeing to a Dominion Status weakened India's resistance to the British presence, he argued.

Jawaharlal Nehru and Subash Chandra Bose became the most prominent youth leaders. They declared that India would give an ultimatum to the British and prepare for mass struggle. Nehru and Bose won the hearts of many Indians. However, Gandhi and other leading Congressmen disapproved Jawaharlal's efforts.

Nevertheless, Jawahar continued organising demonstrations and *hartals*. The demonstrations ended mostly in police *lathi* charge and firing. At Lahore the leading Congressman of Punjab, Lajpat Rai, was severely beaten up. The news of his death triggered agitations throughout India; Jawaharlal arrived in Lucknow and called upon the youth of Lucknow to respond to this challenge.

The boycott committee was given permission to take out a procession on 28 November, but was told to avoid the European shopping area — where the Governor was attending a garden party that day. The organisers said it was too late to alter the route and when the procession started to move, the participants were lathi-charged by mounted police. They refused to permit any more processions. They stopped a group of 12, led by Jawaharlal and Gobind Ballabh Pant, who were proceeding to a public meeting. The police used lathis to disperse them; Jawaharlal also received two blows, but they refused to budge. A huge crowd gathered, and the officials ultimately had to permit Jawaharlal and his companions to proceed to the meeting along their chosen route.

A large procession led by Jawaharlal reached the station and took position at a spot closer to the route of the commission, rather than the one allotted to them. This was close to an open space and the police charged on them — using both lathis and spears, on a crowd of about 30,000 running to about two or three furlongs. Hundreds were beaten up and many trampled upon but the large crowd neither retreated nor retaliated, and stood firm. The police stopped when the commission had passed. Jawaharlal received half a dozen blows on his back, legs and shoulders but was soon surrounded by students who shielded him from further attacks.

The news of the lathi-charge aroused widespread anger in India. It aided the development of national resistance to British rule and also upheld Jawaharlal's national standing. His popularity was on the rise and he was accepted as one of the leaders of his generation. Gandhi appreciated him saying, 'My love to you. It was done bravely.'

Jawaharlal intensified his campaign for complete independence while Gandhi and Motilal favoured Dominion Status. Jawaharlal was in a difficult position. He decided to find a compromise, because of his affection for both of them. Gandhi was also keen to avoid a break up. He said that the British would be given two years' time to grant Dominion Status to India. If they did not, the Congress would launch a national struggle for full political independence. To pacify Jawaharlal, the time-limit was reduced to one year.

The next one year was a year of preparation for Jawaharlal, to face the government. He wanted dedicated young men and women to organise groups of students, peasants and workers and create a mass awareness among them, for the upcoming struggle. The government was worried and contemplated arresting Jawaharlal but did not have any substantial evidence.

On 29 September, 1929, with Gandhi's support, Jawaharlal was elected president of the next session of Congress at Lahore in December. The older members of the Congress were confident that he would support them under Gandhi's persuasion. On the other hand, Jawaharlal's colleagues hoped that he would split the Congress and carry on with his revolutionary programme. Jawaharlal, however, was torn between his loyalty to Gandhi and the Congress on one side, and ideology on the other side. To the surprise of everyone, he decided to be with Gandhi.

The Congress, by now, was committed to independence and civil disobedience. They had only one goal — complete freedom from British domination. The failure of talks with the British caused the Congress session in Lahore to be held in an atmosphere charged with anti-British sentiments. Jawaharlal's presidential address showed both his strength as well as weakness at that stage. His impatience and fierce eagerness for freedom was evident. His wish was to evict the British from India.

During the campaign of civil disobedience, he accepted the leadership of Gandhi and non-violence, but was ready, if need be, to adopt violent methods in future. To Jawaharlal, discipline was more important than revolution. Political freedom was above social and economic change. He was a practical statesman and also a man of glamour and integrity who could retain his followers, including the student community and intelligentsia, within the Congress.

In the Midst of Action

Throughout India, Jawaharlal organised the celebration of 26 January as Independence Day. The working committee authorised Gandhi to organise mass civil disobedience and to boycott law courts and schools. However, Gandhi decided to march to the sea and violate salt laws. Jawaharlal was excited at this law-breaking movement and marched with Gandhi, which left a deep and permanent impression on him. After this experience, he was full of admiration for Gandhi and would never think of breaking away from him, in spite of the difference in their ideologies at times.

On 6 April, Jallianwala Bagh Day, Gandhi manufactured salt and Jawaharlal called out to the nation as a whole to go ahead with mass disobedience. He was in charge of the campaign in Allahabad. He sold packets of contraband salt in the city. He and his wife led a large procession and made salt from a special kind of earth brought for this purpose and sold it. On 14 April Jawaharlal was arrested at Cheoki, a few miles outside Allahabad. He was punished with six months' simple imprisonment for assisting in salt manufacturing.

'Great Day!' he wrote in his pocket diary when he was imprisoned. He was alone in a barrack reserved for dangerous prisoners. It was surrounded by a 15-feet-high wall. It not only cut off any outside contacts but also restricted his view of the sky during the day and the stars during the night — which he used to enjoy when in prison.

He refused any special privileges and often went hungry. He was terribly bored and worked out a meticulous schedule to overcome this. He would get up early in the morning, run a mile beside the main prison wall, followed by a brisk walk of the same distance. He spent the rest of the time mostly spinning, weaving and reading.

Jawaharlal was not given an enough supply of books. So he had to discontinue his letters to Indira, tracing the history of man. In 1928, when Indira was in Mussoorie, he had written to her about the origins of the Earth, the beginnings of life and human pre-history. He had got as far as the formation of classes, religion and the coming of Aryans, when pressures of his public life put a stop to his writing.

Jawaharlal was not totally isolated because a number of convict warders and orderlies were present, apparently to attend on him, and to mainly keep a watch on him. He was not allowed to mix with the other prisoners lest they should carry any messages. Many warders and servants met him everyday to discuss *'swaraj'* with him. Convicts smuggled in 'flowers' for him while one of his attendants brought him mangoes daily. Jawaharlal was very touched by this and wrote, 'The gift is worthy of the Gods. The man is very poor.' Officials of the jail and the town also called on him very often. On 30 June, Motilal Nehru and Syed Mahmud were also imprisoned. Looking after his father now became his main occupation.

Gandhi, meanwhile, was in Yervada jail. The government, hoping to settle the issue of civil disobedience, transported Motilal and Jawaharlal to Yervada for consultations with Gandhi. However, nothing positive resulted from the talks.

A few days later, Motilal was released on grounds of ill-health. Jawaharlal's own term also had come to an end and he was released on 11 October. Immediately, he resumed the Congress presidency. Since the organisation had been banned, he knew he would be arrested. He launched a no-tax campaign. He called upon the Congress committees to organise non-payment of land revenue, rent and income tax. He was arrested the next day and sentenced to two years' rigorous imprisonment. He had been out of prison only for 10 days.

In prison again, he reverted to his regular hobby of reading. He began to write letters to his daughter once again. Since there was no question of getting any reference books, his writing was based on memory and the previous notes he had made. He had amassed a lot of information. He took a lot of trouble in writing those letters, collecting his thoughts and organising them, to suit a young girl of 13. Jawaharlal wrote the history of the world and man, while in prison. Each letter was devoted to one theme or development, starting with Mohenjo-daro and ancient Greece and finally ending with the present times. The letters, written to overcome the monotony of prison life, were spread over almost three years. They were well-written, with no research assistance. These letters were later published as 'Glimpses of World History.' It was an astonishing achievement indeed.

His mind was also focused on the future of the national movement. An economic revolution and the rousing of a mass revolt were on his agenda. He and his companions, breaking the jail rules, organised a three-day fast protesting against the flogging of political prisoners and their harsh treatment in other jails. He was extremely delighted by the news of his wife's arrest on New Year's Day and by her message on the occasion, 'I am happy beyond measure and proud to follow in the footsteps of my husband.' Jawaharlal, however, realised that on the whole the spirit was low and everyone was in a mood for compromise.

Taking advantage of the exhausted mood, the British government was sending feelers suggesting a settlement. Jawaharlal panicked and pleaded with his father to ignore any such statements even if they offered full independence. Motilal was dying and could not offer any guidance to the working committee. Gandhi was being swayed by the suggestions. Jawaharlal wanted to involve the rural areas also in the struggle but this did not appeal to Gandhi. Disagreeing with Gandhi and grief-stricken by his father's death on 6 February, Jawaharlal remained aloof from the discussions.

Gandhi, on his own, negotiated with the Viceroy and entered into a settlement that disappointed Jawaharlal. Gandhi had agreed to withdraw the civil disobedience in return for a few concessions. In spite of his disappointment at the Congress session at Karachi, Jawaharlal approved of the settlement. Though he outwardly supported the political settlement, he knew that it was undoubtedly a self-inflicted defeat. However, he understood that there was no permanent damage to Indian nationalism. Gandhi had, for the time being, ignored the struggle for freedom — which would only end with the attainment of complete independence. This was only a truce. The fight would resume again. He realised that at this moment it was his duty to keep the spirit of battle alive in the hearts of people, and hence support Gandhi's leadership.

Jawaharlal called upon the Congress members not to give up their war mindset and to be prepared to fight again. In the meantime, they should abide by their leader's agreement, but at the same time exploit fully the concessions given in the settlement in sections such as picketing of liquor shops, manufacture of salt, boycott of foreign cloth and use of *swadeshi* goods.

The government, taking note of Gandhi's eagerness to make the settlement a success, sought to create a gap between him and Jawaharlal. They were somewhat successful in their efforts.

Jawaharlal suffered from ill-health at that time and he was forced to take a holiday. It left Gandhi alone in charge of the UP problem. He asked the tenants to pay all the rent they could as soon as possible, as against the earlier no-rent campaign of Jawaharlal. The government set about breaking the alliance of the UP Congress and the tenants. When Jawaharlal returned, he found that the situation had worsened. The *talukdars* were terrorising the peasants with the help of the police. Congress volunteers were beaten up in many places. Even peaceful picketing was banned. Gandhi suggested to the Viceroy that district authorities should fix the rent after consulting with the Congress workers. Jawaharlal urged that since the tenants had already paid some amount, further collections should be suspended. The government did not agree to both. The general attitude of the Government of India stiffened.

Jawaharlal called upon all the branches of the Congress to refrain from any act of civil disobedience for the time being. He publicly denied that the Congress was against the *zamindars* or wanted to create a class war. Gandhi was then in London for the Round Table Conference and Jawaharlal did not want to embarrass him in any way.

Jawaharlal toured the districts. He saw that the conditions in each district depended on the attitude of the local officials. However, on the whole, the situation was serious. He was almost forced to call for a no-rent campaign. He brought the crisis to the notice of the Viceroy and Gandhi. Gandhi allowed Jawaharlal to do as he thought fit.

However, the Government of India was ready for a fight. Discussions of the UP Congress Committee with the officials resulted in nothing concrete. The central and local governments wanted to strengthen forces within the Congress against Jawaharlal. However, Jawaharlal also was not keen to go ahead with the no-rent campaign now, mainly because of Gandhi's absence. Though he tried to project the peasant problem as a struggle against the British, he knew it was part of the class war.

On 6 December, a few district Congress committees were allowed to start their no-rent campaigns. Payment of rent in these districts came to a standstill. Other districts were to follow suit. To strengthen their case, the UP Government lowered the water rates, and introduced a bill to stop eviction of tenants if they have paid 2/3 arrears of the dues. Jawaharlal and other leaders were not permitted to speak or write in support of the campaign.

Finally, Jawaharlal was arrested on 26 December for violating the order that did not allow him to move out of Allahabad. He was arrested when he was in train, on his way to Bombay to welcome Gandhi.

Life in Prison

Jawahar's prison life started affecting him. His general health deteriorated and he had problems with his teeth. He was first put in Naini jail but after a few weeks, was transferred to Bareilly. He lived there under discomfort and the men were also cruel. His ward and the barracks were at least six feet below ground level, and were locked at night. His meeting with the family was monitored and a policeman took notes of the conversation.

Other atrocities added to his frustrations. In April, his mother was beaten up in a lathi-charge and was badly injured. Once, during an interrogation, the jailor insulted Jawaharlal's mother and wife who were also present. The government ordered that Jawaharlal should not be interrogated for a month. He was angry and refused to meet anyone even after a month, as he did not want his mother and wife to be insulted again. It was after a break of eight months, in 1933, that he began to see visitors—that too under Gandhi's persuasion.

In June 1932, he was shifted to Dehra Dun jail where the atmosphere was much more pleasant. The superintendent, an Irishman by name Captin Falvey, was very kind to him. Jawaharlal was allowed to walk outside the prison gates. However, the news of ill-treatment of prisoners in other jails caused him great mental stress. He felt sorry for them and did not like his being under better conditions.

He was also worried about his mother and wife who were on their own, and his two sisters who were languishing in jail. Above all, he missed his daughter. It was because his letters brought her closer to him and so he continued with letter-writing. There was no restriction this time round in prison, on the number of books he could read and keep. He was also given newspapers and journals.

In the meantime, Gandhi commenced a fast in 1932, when it was announced that people belonging to the scheduled caste would be treated as a separate community for election purposes. This shocked Jawaharlal, for he was scared that Gandhi might die. He was the only protective force in Jawaharlal's life at that time, and the very thought of losing him upset him tremendously. He wept in anger and love, and wondered how Gandhi could create such a situation so carelessly. He was bitter towards the people who forced others to risk their lives in such a way. Sensing Jawaharlal's reaction Gandhi sent him a telegram, which gave him the news of his breaking the fast, and only then did Jawaharlal stabilise.

The next year Gandhi undertook a fast again, which sent Jawaharlal and millions of his countrymen into despair. Gandhi wrote a letter to soothe him. Jawaharlal's reply indicated his bewilderment and dread of personal loss. At the beginning of the fast, the government released Gandhi who suspended civil disobedience for six weeks. This came as a big blow to Jawaharlal but he accepted it.

On 30 August, 12 days before Jawaharlal was scheduled to be out of prison, he was released. On emerging from jail, he made comments that he attached no importance to the *swadeshi* and Harijan movements. He added that India's primary problem was economic, and a new society was inevitable. He wanted to combine national struggle with socialism. His difference of opinion gave the impression that he would break away from Gandhi and the Congress, and form a new party with the prime goal of independence.

Gandhi wanted to renew peace negotiations with the British and wanted to reform his countrymen by way of fasting. His methods were the politics of intuition, needing no argument or logic. Jawaharlal followed the path of reason, applying the laws of history and change. So the break was certain.

When Jawaharlal went to Pune to meet his leader, he was mentally prepared for it. However, he knew that in the political struggle, Gandhi's leadership was indispensable. Congress was the only revolutionary organisation in India. He needed both the leader and the party. So Jawaharlal once again accepted Gandhi's leadership. Though he disagreed with Gandhi in private conversation, to the outside world he was determined to accept Congress's policy and decisions.

Travelling around the country, Jawaharlal realised that bitterness against the government and the desire to bring it down were at its peak. He wanted to keep communalism out of it, and wanted to strengthen the national struggle by making it a social and economic battle for the masses. Hindu and Muslim communalists, however, wanted no basic change in the political and economic structure, and with official favours, tried to better their own position. They were anti-national, but he rebuked them mildly.

However, his public activities did not last long. All the local governments were given orders to arrest him on a serious charge whenever the opportunity arose. What worried the government was the impact of his speeches and writings on the lower middle classes. Being very poor, they might accept his new revolutionary theories. On his visit to Calcutta in January, he spoke to the masses disapproving imperialism. He was arrested and sentenced to two years' simple imprisonment.

In Alipore Central Jail in Calcutta, he got accustomed to the routine prison life — living in a small cell and a bare barrack. A clerk, who was sentenced for fraud, was his only companion. He finished reading all the books available at the prison library. He could not settle down there, and was relieved when he was shifted to the Dehra Dun jail.

Throughout these months, he was worried about the ill-health of his mother and wife. There was no cheerful news from the political front also. Gandhi's withdrawal of the Civil Disobedience Movement hit him hard. He felt it was an insult to the nation and the thought of parting ways surfaced in his mind once again.

In August, Kamala's condition worsened and he was let out of prison. Taking this opportunity, he wrote a letter to Gandhi, but Gandhi did not take it seriously. After 11 days when Kamala's health improved, Jawaharlal was taken back to prison. This time round, he was put in Naini jail and was allowed to see Kamala once or twice a week. When she was moved to a sanatorium in Bowali in October, he was shifted to a nearby jail in Almora.

His life was now fully focused on Kamala's illness and everything else took a backseat. Over the years, their relationship had developed from indifference to one of deep attachment. In jail, he often thought of her, waited for her letters and looked forward to her visits. With death knocking at her door, he was nervous and frantically worried. To clear his mind off these unpleasant thoughts, he put his mind to work totally — writing his life story. He began writing in June 1934 and completed it on 14 February 1935. It was a massive manuscript of 976 pages, finished in less than nine months, and turned out to be his greatest literary achievement.

Meanwhile, Kamala's condition was not improving and it was decided that she should be taken to Europe. For the first time, Jawaharlal was worried about money. He had an annual income of about Rs. 9,000 with which he had to run a huge establishment in Anand Bhavan, pay medical bills, arrange for sea transport and stay in Europe. A member of the Birla family (a wealthy financier), on hearing about his difficulties, offered him a monthly allowance (as it was done for many other leading Congressmen). Jawaharlal was surprised at the suggestion and refused the offer. He somehow made arrangements with his own savings and Kamala set sail with Indira and a doctor attending on Kamala, in May.

Death of Kamala Nehru

When Kamala's condition became critical in September, Nehru's sentence was suspended so that he would be able to be by her side. 'So this is the end,' he wrote in his diary. Kamala was in a clinic in the Black Forest region in Germany. She had become physically and mentally weak. She was anxious to get back to Switzerland and so Jawaharlal shifted her to a clinic in Lausanne. Her condition fluctuated daily and Jawaharlal hoped against hope; but on 28 February, at 5 am, she breathed her last.

The publication of Jawaharlal's Autobiography, a few weeks after the death of Kamala, gave an inkling of his feelings — and the world shared his sorrow. The book was highly acclaimed all over the world. It was an essential document of the period, giving glimpses of the ideas and politics of a whole new world.

The West could understand this man who spoke and thought with a modern outlook and reason. In his book, Jawaharlal showed that in India nationalism was a civilised and responsible movement, based on the principles of European revolution and liberalism. The book became an instant sell-out, running into many editions within weeks.

The entire book was written in prison. His happy marriage and its tragic end were revealed in a few words of dedication, 'To Kamala, who is no more.'

Writing was a form of solace for him. He however had no bitterness against the British. Jawaharlal's quarrel was not with the British but with imperialism, capitalism and with the social evils of religion. After his wife's death, he returned to India. He immersed himself in work to overcome the vacuum in his heart.

As the Leader of the Party

When Jawaharlal was in Europe, he had been elected president of the Congress for the year 1936. The decision was mainly that of Gandhi. The main issue before the Congress was whether they should contest the elections and accept office in the provinces under the new Government of India Act 1935. A majority was for acceptance of office. However, Jawaharlal was not in favour of the act. Any firm decision, however, was to be taken only after the elections. The working committee agreed with Jawaharlal that a close association had to be developed between the masses and the Congress organisation.

In his presidential address, Jawaharlal analysed the world's situation and India's place in it. He said that the national movement should draw strength and inspiration from the masses. Congress should not only be for the masses, but of the masses. According to him, the only solution of the world's problems and India's poverty and deprivation lay in socialism.

Jawaharlal stayed out of the elections but started a country-wide campaign in Bombay, with a bang. The Congress was contesting the elections and trying to gain entry into the assemblies in order to make the Act not viable. He felt that acceptance of office would weaken their movement. His forceful socialist ideal caused resentment. So, opposition against him in the Congress increased. They appealed to Gandhi who in turn asked Jawaharlal to explain. He stuck to his opinion, and was criticised by others vehemently, following which he offered to resign. However, Gandhi pulled him up for arrogance, intolerance and lack of sense of humour.

Jawaharlal was indispensable to the Congress Party as the party was to him. His election tours and speeches made him very popular and got the support of a large number of radical youth. There were many men and women in India, with a patriotic feeling, who saw in Jawaharlal the spokesman of their viewpoint. He was the only Indian politician who had an international audience. He was able to get the party recognition on the world stage.

Jawaharlal now directed all his energies towards winning the elections. This was the first of his national campaigns.

He covered the villages by train, plane, car, cycle, cart and steamer, on horse, elephant and camel and on foot. Once he even ran for half a mile to reach a meeting place, with the crowd following him. Another time the audience was so large that he had to walk on their shoulders! There was in him a kind of spontaneity and vitality that endeared him to the masses.

The schedule started at dawn and went on till late in the night, and on one occasion for 24 hours without a break. He talked about the common problem affecting the Indian people — poverty, debt and foreign rule — and made them think of India as a whole. Many had no interest in all this. They merely came to see the god-like figure about whom they had heard so much. Gandhi was one of them but Jawaharlal was the 'glamorous prince.'

World War II and India

When World War II broke out, the Viceroy, without consulting the people's representatives, declared war on the Axis powers, on behalf of India. According to Jawaharlal, it was for India to decide whether she would go to war. India should be given freedom if she was to participate in the war. The government was not willing, and the Congress ministries in the provinces resigned.

Jawaharlal Nehru remained sympathetic towards the British cause. He joined Maulana Azad, C. Rajagopalachari and Patel in offering Congress support to the war, if the British agreed to grant independence after the war.

The response of the government was not favourable. The Congress again accepted the leadership of Gandhi and prepared for the conflict. The government continued to arrest the Congress leaders and Jawaharlal expected his detention any time.

Gandhi's stand was non-violence, and a demand for freedom of speech to preach against participation in the war. The demand would be shown by individual civil disobedience. Vinoba Bhave would first make a public speech against the war and court arrest. Next it was going to be Nehru's turn.

Jawaharlal proceeded to Wardha to prevent Gandhi from observing a fast unto death in protest against the British stubbornness. Jawaharlal was arrested on 30 October at Cheoki station on his way back to Allahabad. He was sentenced for four years, much to the surprise of everyone. Churchill directed the Viceroy not to treat Jawaharlal as an ordinary criminal and hoped his sentence would be modified, but in vain. After a week in Gorakhpur jail, Jawaharlal Nehru was stealthily moved at night to the Dehra Dun jail. He remained there till the end of 1941.

Life in jail was not easy for Jawaharlal. He was given one weekly newspaper and six books to read, at a given point of time. He could have only one visitor, send one letter and receive one every fortnight. He was not allowed a washer-man or a barber and other prisoners were not permitted to talk to him. No one was allowed to send him food packets and other essential items. He could get nothing from home and once he did not even have toothpaste.

All letters sent to him by his daughter and others lay piled up in the office. After a while the letters that came from his daughter were handed over to him. Later, he was allowed to write letters on the condition that none of those will be published. Jawaharlal refused to agree to any condition. Instead, he gave up letter-writing altogether and depended on visitors to keep in touch with the outside world. Indira, who returned to India in May, took a cottage near Mussorie, and this made Jawaharlal happy.

It was during this period that he dwelt on the 5,000 years of India's history. While on his election tours, he had glimpses of the myriad features of India's diverse unity. He learnt to appreciate India's thought and culture. He had earlier dreamt of an India of the 20th century. This dream was still there, but now carried with it a sense pride in India's achievements.

By the end of the year, the government decided to release all Congressmen from jail and Nehru was free again, on December 4. Gandhiji formally withdrew from the AICC and proclaimed Jawaharlal as his chosen successor.

The Japanese, in the meantime, were drawing close to the Indian shores. The Congress, under the leadership of Gandhi and Nehru, appealed to the people to remain calm, be prepared for air raids, maintain law and order, set up co-operatives to ensure food supplies, and resist the Japanese to the best of their abilities.

The British sent Cripps with the proposals of a dominion constitution rather than full independence. However, the Cripps mission failed.

Gandhi had no clear-cut idea as to how the British should be forced to quit India. Jawaharlal was against a mass Civil Disobedience Movement. At the Bombay AICC, the leaders called for the British to 'Quit India.' Gandhi was authorised to start a non-violent mass struggle, if the power was not transferred to Indian hands. Gandhi wanted to make every effort to see the Viceroy.

The response of the government was to trap the leaders of the Congress in their homes. Jawaharlal was arrested along with the entire Congress Committee. He served the longest term in prison (over 34 months), from 9 August, 1942 to 15 June, 1945. The 12 members of the Congress Committee lived together in Ahmednagar till March 1945. Then they were dispersed and sent to different places.

Forced to stay in close quarters, and being away from home and the news of the death of dear ones frayed the nerves of the Congress members who very often indulged in heated discussions. At the end of it all, they were hardly on speaking terms. To smoothen out the friction, Jawaharlal organised a regular community life. Duties were allotted to each person. He himself did a lot of work — supervising the cooking, preparing salads, nursing the sick, organising badminton and volley ball matches and taking charge of gardening.

When books and journals were allowed, Jawaharlal found comfort in them. On 13 April, 1944 he re-started the writing of the book he had begun in Dehra Dun jail. Within five months, *The Discovery of India*, about a thousand hand-written pages, was completed. The book is a detailed survey of India's culture prior to the British rule.

Jawaharlal and his companions were in a bitter mood when they were freed from prison. The conditions in India were pitiable. The Bengal famine, rampant corruption and black marketing were grossly neglected. Jawaharlal's speeches reflected his anger at the state of affairs. Gandhi was planning another mass Civil Disobedience Movement. The British refused to regard Congress as a non-Hindu secular organisation and were bent on creating a rift between the Hindus and the Muslims. By 1946, the air was filled with hatred and excitement, which led to widespread riots and killing.

In August 1946, the Viceroy invited Jawaharlal, as president of the Congress, to submit proposals for the interim government, with co-operation from Jinnah, the leader of the Muslim League. But the talks between Nehru and Jinnah failed. However, the Congress insisted on a ministry of 14 members, including Hindus, Muslims and other minorities. The ministry would function as a strong and stable government. Later, the League also joined the interim government.

The developments in different parts of India were disturbing. Hindus were slaughtered in Bengal. In retaliation, Muslims were killed in Bihar. Gandhi and Jawaharlal urged the Congress ministry to deal strictly with the guilty, and received the support of the Viceroy and the League in this matter. Jawaharlal and one of the League ministers toured the affected districts and brought the situation under control. The full credit for such firm and decisive action goes to Jawaharlal. Nehru did this in his own capacity.

Meanwhile, the interim government was weakened by disputes and arguments. Both the groups were engaged in a battle of wits. By the end of January 1947, it was clear that negotiations and compromises were not possible. The Congress threatened to leave the government if the League continued to hold office in the interim government. However, the British government announced that the British would leave India not later than June 1948.

India's First Prime Minister

On 24 March, 1947, Lord Mountbatten was sworn in as the Viceroy. Jawaharlal Nehru and his colleagues were anxious for quick and final decisions on the transfer of power. The Congress held a presidential election. Its chosen leader would become India's head of the government. Eleven Congress units suggested Vallabhai Patel while only the working committee nominated Nehru. Gandhi, however, supported Nehru and asked Patel to withdraw. Nehru thus headed the interim government.

Difficult times followed. Communal fury spread intensely; Lahore was being burnt while Calcutta was faced with another round of killings. The Muslim League, led by Mohammad Ali Jinnah, was demanding a separate Muslim state of Pakistan. The British officials were either not willing or incapable to deal with the situation.

Under pressure from the Congress, the British decided to bring forward the date of the transfer of power to 1947 itself. Jawaharlal Nehru hoped that the communal frenzy would die down once the decision on Pakistan was taken. However, all were surprised and startled by the widespread and savage killings that distraught India before and after the partition. After 2 June, Jawaharlal Nehru's thoughts were fully devoted to the future.

At midnight on 14 August, 1947, the Constituent Assembly met to usher in the dawn of freedom. Jawaharlal once again made a brilliant speech, that was moving and appropriate for the occasion.

'Long years ago we made a tryst with destiny and now the time comes, when we shall redeem our pledge not wholly or in full measure, but very substantially. At the stroke of the midnight hour, when the world sleeps, India will awake to life and freedom.'

When trouble started on August 14, the reaction was one of surprise and helplessness. A large number of people were killed. Nehru moved around Delhi, personally protecting the frightened Muslim families. To stop rioters, he jumped into the midst of the frantic mob, and at times even hit them, and tried to suppress the trouble.

Nehru addressed meetings, proclaiming that Congress was always a secular party and they should all work together to build an India, where every citizen could live freely, without any fear, whatever be his religion.

Nehru, working in such a turbulent atmosphere, again grew very close to Gandhi and depended on him more than ever. Gandhi supported Nehru's efforts to safeguard the minorities, quell violence and fight the narrow-minded outlook, which was becoming dominant. The violence hurt Nehru deeply and he called for a ceasefire and the UN intervention, to stop the Indo-Pakistan war of 1947. Patel was not in favour of this and Gandhi too gave his consent reluctantly.

Nehru asserted his own control over the Kashmir policy while Patel disapproved Nehru's action of not consulting the Home Ministry. Patel wanted to withdraw from the scene because a political battle at this juncture would be bad for India. However, Gandhi, on 30 January, 1948, told Patel not to leave the government and to continue being in a joint leadership with Nehru. A free India, according to Gandhi, desperately needed both Nehru and Patel.

Gandhi was assassinated on 30 January, 1948. The personal blow this caused to Nehru was overwhelming. Rushing to Birla House on hearing the news, he sobbed like a child. However, a few hours later, when he addressed the nation, his voice was calm.

Nehru and Patel embraced each other and addressed the nation together. Patel's Home Ministry was criticised by the media and other politicians for not protecting Gandhi. Taking moral responsibility, Patel offered to resign. Nehru, however, dismissed any such move. He reminded Patel of their working partnership of 30 years in the freedom struggle. It was not right for them to quarrel after Gandhi's death. Consoled, Patel publicly endorsed Nehru's leadership. But despite their working together, both of them had differences of opinion on various issues.

Nehru put pressure on Dr. Rajendra Prasad to refuse his nomination to become the First President of India in 1950, in order to favour Rajagopalachari. This angered the party, which felt that Nehru was imposing his will. Even Patel did not support him and Rajendra Prasad was elected.

Many such incidents took place, where Nehru wanted to have his own way but was prevented, and faced stiff resistance. Patel knew that Nehru had to understand that his will was not law with the Congress. But when Nehru offered to resign, he personally prevented him from doing so because Patel felt that the party had no confidence in him.

Leading India

After independence, it was his daughter who looked after him and managed his personal affairs. Patel died in 1950 and Nehru became the most popular and powerful Indian politician. Under his leadership, the Congress won a thumping victory in the elections of 1952 and his son-in-law Feroz Gandhi was also elected to the Parliament. Indira stayed with Nehru in his official residence to look after him, thereby estranging her husband — who criticised the Nehru government. Indira, nevertheless, continued to be his constant companion in all his affairs, including his travels in India and abroad.

Nehru believed in social equality and looked with admiration towards USSR. He implemented his socialist vision by creating the Planning Commission of India. He drew up the first five-year plan in 1951, which streamlined the government's investments in industries and agriculture. He increased business and income taxes. The government would manage industries such as mining, electricity and heavy industries. He introduced a policy of land distribution and started programmes to build irrigation canals, dams and the use of fertilizers, to increase agricultural production. Cottage industries were also given a boost to improve rural life. Nehru also launched a programme to harness nuclear energy.

During his tenure as the Prime Minister, he had to deal with serious food shortages. In spite of the overwhelming industrial growth, production, quality and profit did not meet the expectations. There was persistent unemployment and poverty. Nehru's popularity was still on the rise and his government was successful in extending electricity and water supply, health care and roads to a vast population in the rural areas.

Nehru wished to combine Indian traditions with Western technology. He had great plans and dreams for India. Jawaharlal was a passionate advocate of education for the country's progress in future. His vision resulted in the establishment of many institutions of higher learning such as the All India Institute of Medical Sciences, The Indian Institute of Technology and the Indian Institute of Management. Free and compulsory education for all children was introduced in primary classes. Free milk and meals were provided to children to combat malnutrition. Vocational and technical schools, and adult education centres were also started in the rural areas.

Jawaharlal also brought about many changes in the Hindu law to penalise caste discrimination and increase the legal rights and freedom of women. A system of reservation in government jobs and educational institutions helped in eradicating the social inequalities faced by the scheduled castes and tribes.

It was Nehru who pioneered the policy of non-alignment and founded the Non-Aligned Movement of nations showing neutrality between the rival nations led by the United States and the USSR. He worked to defuse global tensions and the threat of nuclear weapons. However, his miscalculations on the military ability of China brought about India's defeat in the Indo-Chinese war in October 1962.

Nehru led the Congress to a major victory in the 1957 elections. Problems and criticism of the government were on the rise. Disillusioned by internal bickering and rising corruption, he wanted to resign but still continued to serve. The election of his daughter to the post of the Congress president in 1959 drew a lot of criticism. China's antagonism grew when Nehru gave asylum to Dalai Lama. On the other hand, his military action to free Goa from Portugal increased his popularity.

In 1962, he led the Congress to victory, but with lesser majority. All the opposition parties had performed better. On 6 January 1964, at the Congress session held at Bhubaneswar, Nehru suffered a mild stroke on the left side. After a short period of rest, he resumed his work as usual. He knew that his end was not far off. On his table lay the lines of Robert Frost, copied out. It shows that though tired, his sense of duty to his people was foremost in his mind.

> *The woods are lovely, dark and deep,*
> *But I have promises to keep,*
> *And miles to go before I sleep,*
> *And miles to go before I sleep.*

He cleared all his pending papers, dealt with his correspondence and went to bed. In the early hours of May 27, he suffered a rupture of the abdominal aorta. Pain-killing injections had to be administered to him to induce sleep, from which he never woke up again.

Jawaharlal Nehru was a charismatic and sensitive political leader. He remained true to his ideals till the very end. As the first Prime Minister of Independent India, he visualised a developed, modern India and worked diligently towards achieving this dream. He will always be remembered as one of the most loved, admired and respected leaders of modern India.

Prodigy books

Biographies

Abdul Kalam
Charles Darwin
Marie Curie
Visvesvaraya
Srinivasa Ramanujan
Newton
Einstein
James Watt
Jagdish Chandra Bose
Alexander Graham Bell
Gandhi
Jawaharlal Nehru
Mother Teresa
Ambedkar
Bhagat Sigh
Tipu Sultan
Rani of Jhansi
Akbar
Shivaji
Bharati
Martin Luther King
Alexander the Great
Napoleon
Adolf Hitler
Charlie Chaplin
Walt Disney
Bill Gates
Narayana Murthy

Classics Retold

Homer's Iliad
The Odyssey
The Tempest
Hamlet
The Merchant of Venice
Twelfth Night
Romeo and Juliet
Macbeth

Other Titles

The Universe
Hinduism
Global Warming
Abraham Lincoln
The New 7 wonders of the World
Life
Tsunami
Dinosaurs
Ganga
World War II
Madras - Chennai
Exam Tips
The Internet